Healing Crystals
A Guide to Working with
Obsidian

Brenda Hunt

copyright © Brenda Hunt 2013
All rights reserved world wide
No part of 'Healing Crystals - A Guide to Working with
Obsidian' may be reproduced or stored by any means
without the express permission of Brenda Hunt

Whilst reasonable care is taken to ensure the accuracy
of the information in this publication, no responsibility can
be accepted for the consequences of any actions based on
any opinions, information or advice found in the publication.

Healing information contained in this publication should
not be taken as a substitute for professional medical advice.
You should always consult your doctor on serious matters.

ISBN-13: 978-1482647075
ISBN-10: 1482647079

Contents

Introduction

This report has been written to introduce you to working with the healing energies of the beautiful gemstone obsidian, but of course you do also need some more general information about working with healing crystals, especially if this is one of your first crystals.

What is crystal healing?

When we talk about crystals in crystal healing we are talking about semiprecious gemstones rather than the manmade glass crystals that are often used in jewellery and ornaments. The crystals that we use for their healing energies are the crystalline forms of minerals, and most of them are beautiful.

You will be familiar with many of them from the world of jewellery.

Citrine, rock crystal or clear quartz, sapphire, emerald, tourmaline, tigers, eye, rose quartz, peridot, garnet and of course, obsidian

All of these gemstones and many more have different healing energies that can help balance your energy field and help to heal you.

They work on different layers of our energy field - the spiritual, the emotional, the mental and the physical. You can work with single crystals or with many at the same time.

You can set aside time to create healing layouts or you can simply wear or carry them with you every day.

Healing crystals can be used by anyone in almost any situation. You can even work with healing crystals to help your pets and animals. I work with rose quartz to help rescue animals regain their confidence and trust of humans.

Although the idea of working with crystals for their healing properties may sound strange, in fact we work with the energy of crystals every day without even thinking about it. The quartz movement in your watch is a paper thin piece of quartz, which vibrates in response to an electric charge from the battery and allows the watch to keep good time.

This Piezoelectric property in quartz has been crucial to many of our technological advances, not only watches but the computer chip, lasers, communication systems, ultrasound, and our entertainment systems are based on the quartz crystal.

We are happy to work with the healing energies of metals and crystals when it is approved of by science and the establishment. For instance, the antimicrobial and antibacterial properties of silver means that it is often impregnated into bandages and plasters.

Although this report will give you some general information about crystal healing, in the main it is specifically about the healing energies of the beautiful black gemstone obsidian.

It is one of a series of reports, each one of which focuses on a specific crystal or crystal family.

Obsidian

Chemical formula: SiO_2 + Fe_2O_3 + H_2O + Al,C,Ca,K,Na,Fe
Crystal system: Amorphous
Mohs scale: hardness 5 to 5.5
Mineral group: oxide
Colour: Black, Brown, rainbow, Sheen
Sources: Mexico, USA, worldwide
Chakra: root chakra
Zodiac: Capricorn, libra, scorpio

Obsidian is a beautiful, mystical and mysterious, intense black gemstone that is formed volcanically when lava cools rapidly during a volcanic explosion.

It is created when lava hardens so fast that no crystalline structures are able to form, so obsidian is an amorphous crystal, which means a solidified molten mass, a volcanic glass.

It is a gemstone that holds the power of a volcano, a power that is destructive and creative at the same time, one of the most incredible powers of Mother Earth.

It is a wonderful gemstone to work with, bringing the ability of a volcano to destroy, change and create a landscape into your energy life. Grounding, protective, insightful and supportive, it can be a powerful energy for change, helping you deal with deep-seated problems, even those that go back to a past life.

It is a strongly protective crystal protecting you not only from your own negative energies but the negative energies of others that surround you, creating your own personal shield against the effects that other people can have on you.

As well as being powerfully protective, obsidian is also a beautiful gemstone. The black glass of obsidian has a shine like no other gem, while rainbow and Sheen obsidian have fascinating plays of subtle colour, which makes them particularly good for spiritual work, meditation and scrying. Snowflake obsidian is a very unusual black and white gemstone, very popular for jewellery, the white markings in are formed by feldspar crystals inside the black obsidian

Most obsidian is opaque but Apache tears (smoky obsidian) and Lamellen Obsidian (also called Midnight Lace Obsidian) are transparent. They form when there are no foreign substances in the mix.

Obsidian in history

Obsidian was used to create some of the most ancient artefacts used by mankind and has been found in archaeological sites all around the world.

The gem is apparently named after the Roman Obsius, who - according to Pliny – was said to have brought the first gems to Rome from Ethiopia.

Because of the nature of obsidian - it has a very glassy lustre - it can be made into mirrors and this quality of the gemstone was used by ancient civilisations to create scrying mirrors which were used for divination. The Mayan priests of the God Tetzcatlipoca (smoking Mirror) used obsidian mirrors to predict the future, and that is only one example of the way many ancient peoples worked with the mystical energies of this gem.

Obsidian's lack of a crystal structure, means that obsidian blade edges can be cut to incredible thinness, which meant that it could be formed into sharp edges, leading to its ancient use as arrowheads and blades.

Obsidian blades have been found from burials as early as Paleolithic times and the sacrificial knives of the Aztecs were made from obsidian. Many obsidian tools have been found in locations far from the source of the gem, showing how important it was in ancient times. In fact, obsidian tools have been found in sites dating back at least 14,000 years and across the globe, in Europe, the Middle East, the Americas, even on Easter Island in the Pacific.

Indeed, obsidian scalpel blades are used in cardiac surgery, as they have a cutting edge that is many times sharper than high-quality steel. Even the best metal knife has jagged edges when seen under a strong enough microscope, but even seen an under an electron microscope, an obsidian blade is still smooth and even, they also produce less scarring than a traditional scalpel.

Choosing your obsidian

You read a lot about choosing healing crystals, some of it makes it sound very complicated.

Many books and people will talk about the way that the crystal chooses you, which can make it sound as if you have to wait around until a crystal leaps out at you shouting "choose me, choose me". They will also talk about having to choose a crystal that has the right energy for you.

Of course both of these ideas are true, but it can sound very daunting to anyone who is new to crystal healing.

In fact, there is nothing complicated about it at all.

You will find that you are simply attracted to the right crystal. It will capture your attention, because it looks pretty or it's a lovely colour or a comforting shape, it will just catch your eye. And as far as having the right energy, it will simply feel right, feel comfortable in your hand. Sometimes you just won't want to put it down again in the shop - when that happens, you know it's the right crystal for you.

But you don't actually have to pick a crystal up to know it's the right one. You don't even have to be in the same room as it, or the same country for that matter. One of my own personal favourite crystals, a piece that I work with all the time, came to me from the other side of the world. It was on a website, not even a healing website, a gemstone one for the jewellery trade, and as soon as I saw the photo, I knew it was a crystal for me.

You also have to take into account where you are buying a crystal from. A lot of shops and websites sell crystals purely as a product, without any knowledge of their healing energies apart from the leaflets that they come with.

You may still find a crystal that calls to you in a gift shop, but you will normally find it easier to find crystals with clean, clear energy if you deal with specialists who understand the crystals, their healing energies and how to work with them.

Don't be afraid to buy online. As long as you feel comfortable with the website and the people you are buying from, the right crystals tend to find their way to you.

What form of crystal should you choose?

You can choose your crystals in their natural unpolished form or polished (tumbled). You can choose small pieces (less than 1 inch across) to keep close to you in some way, or large pieces to place somewhere in your room, or you can choose them as jewellery or carvings, keyrings, paperweights, healing wands or dowsing pendulums

There is no right or wrong type.

It depends entirely on how you want to work with them and what suits you.

The only thing that is wrong is choosing a piece of healing crystal purely on someone else's advice, a piece that you don't really feel comfortable with.

Once you get it home you'll find that you don't actually work with it. It will sit on a shelf, or worse still, in a drawer, hidden from sight and mind.

For instance, you might buy a piece of jewellery that you're not comfortable with. A style that deep in your heart, you know you won't be comfortable wearing. There's no point in buying a beautiful Obsidian arrowhead strung on a leather cord as a pendant when you always wear dainty silver set jewellery. You might wear it for a few days, but eventually you will revert to your preferred style of jewellery and the beautiful but too chunky piece will sit in your jewellery box. The same thing will happen with any piece that doesn't suit your personal choice and style.

Is bigger better?

Will a great big heavy chunk of obsidian do you more good than a small delicate piece?

No.

When a crystal is inside your energy field, the actual size of it doesn't matter, so it isn't a case of more is more. A simple pair of obsidian ear studs or a small tumbled stone in your pocket will work as well as a large bead necklace or a large natural piece of obsidian on your desk in front of you.

As long as it is close to you the size won't affect the energy you feel.

The exception to this is when you want the obsidian to improve the energy of a larger space, a room or work area. If the crystal needs to energise a larger area, or you want to keep a piece further away from you — somewhere in the room or in your work area, but not within arm's length — then you will need a larger piece so that it has enough energy to fill a larger area. Choose a large natural piece at least 4" (10cm) across.

If you want to create a barrier against negative energy with your obsidian, you can literally form a barrier, almost a wall by placing wither a larger piece or a line of smaller pieces between you and the source of the negative energy. If you want it to be less visually obvious, collect some carvings or pieces that you can use as paperweights – a line of tumbled stones on your desk can lead to some questions!

The golden rule in choosing your crystal is to make sure that you like it.

So when you're choosing your obsidian, or any crystal, trust your instincts.

In fact, that's one of the most important lessons in working with crystals - learn to trust your instincts and obsidian can help you develop this ability, giving you to confidence to trust your `gut' reaction

Working with obsidian?

There is nothing magical about working with obsidian or indeed any healing crystal.

You don't have to do anything to them, you don't have to buy crystals that have been specially treated, had spells cast over them, been infused with Reiki energy or anything else beyond your own personal ability to choose and work with the right crystals.

You are working with the energy of the crystal itself. They are the crystalline forms of the minerals that we need for health, and that we get through the food chain from the earth - although of course you should never eat the actual crystal.

For instance malachite contains copper, howlite includes calcium, obsidian contains iron and the piezoelectric property of quartz has been used by industry and technology for many years. It is involved in the huge variety of everyday items such as the gas lighter, quartz watch, the autofocus on your camera and of course the silicon chip, powering almost everything we use nowadays.

So, as a general rule you really just need to have your choice of crystal close to you, inside your own electromagnetic field, about arm's-length around you. A good guide is your feeling of what is 'your space' when someone gets too physically close to you.

The crystal doesn't actually need to touch your skin, although there is nothing wrong with this with most crystals and obsidian is one of the crystals where it actually can be more effective if it is in contact with your skin.

There are some crystals that are toxic such as unpolished malachite, and you should take care with these crystals, not keeping them in contact with the skin.

Most of the crystals you will actually come across are perfectly safe. A good crystal book will give you information about the crystals you should take care with.

Obsidian is safe in any of its forms - natural, polished or carved, as cabochons or beads set into jewellery, although you should remember that it is a form of glass and take a certain amount of care with it to avoid chipping it.

You can buy some crystal items that are designed to be touched, such as palm stones which are flat, smooth, polished pieces of crystal, often with a groove on the surface to rub your thumb against.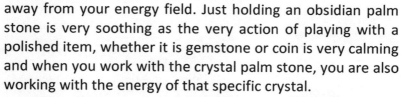

Working with an obsidian palm stone is a very protective experience, as it can help deflect negative energy away from your energy field. Just holding an obsidian palm stone is very soothing as the very action of playing with a polished item, whether it is gemstone or coin is very calming and when you work with the crystal palm stone, you are also working with the energy of that specific crystal.

The way you work with your obsidian will depend to a certain extent on the size and style that you have chosen.

Obviously, if you have chosen a piece of jewellery you will wear it. A tumbled stone or palm stone will probably be in your pocket and a large piece of obsidian will be on a desk or an ornament in your living room.

Obsidian is one of those gemstones that you will probably have in various different forms, because it is so useful and because it is a beautiful natural gemstone that lends itself to many different forms and styles.

Creating an elixir

Although you'll work with the actual crystal in most forms of crystal healing and obsidian is no exception, there are times when it can be useful to create an elixir of the gemstone.

An elixir is a useful way to work with the energy of the healing crystal in situations where you may prefer not to use an actual gemstone, such as working with animals or young children.

You must take care when making an elixir. Some crystals can be destroyed by water and a few are toxic and must only be made using a special method that does not allow physical contact between the crystal and the water.

Obsidian is an excellent crystal for an elixir, it is safe to use, and it will not be damaged by the water.

Making a general elixir is simple. Place your obsidian – a polished tumbled stone is best - into a clear glass container of purified or spring water. You can also use distilled water, which does not contain any energy signature of its own.

It's important to use a clear container as a coloured glass container would affect the elixir, adding colour energy to it.

Place the glass or jug in the sunlight for about three hours during the early morning, or in moonlight overnight.

It's best to cover the container with a piece of white muslin or kitchen towel to keep your elixir clean.

Remove the obsidian before you use the elixir. The energy of the obsidian has been infused into the elixir and you don't want to risk anyone swallowing the actual crystal!

When you use an elixir, you are 'filling' yourself with the energy of the obsidian, and it can be very powerful. So you should always start by drinking small doses throughout the day, rather than a single full glass. The elixir is absorbed faster the more the body needs the energy.

I prefer to make the elixir and use it fresh but if you do want to store it for a few days make sure that you keep it in a cool dark place and away from any strong energies.

Working with an elixir.

Once you've made your elixir, you can of course simply drink it, but there are other ways of working with any gem Elixir.

- Add a few drops to a plain massage oil.
- Rub a few drops onto your hands, then hold them in front of your nose and inhale deeply.
- Massage drops onto your temple before meditating.
- Add a few drops to your bathwater.
- Put a few drops in your washing machine.

Elixir cream

You can also add the elixir to a body cream. Find an un-perfumed cream as pure from additives as you can, and mix a few drops of your elixir into a small pot of this cream.

It is then best to keep the cream in a cool area, possibly the fridge. You can then use this to ease pain or tension by rubbing the cream onto the affected area.

An elixir cream of obsidian is particularly useful for easing the discomfort of Reynauds Disease, where blood flow to the fingers and toes can be blocked temporarily, causing discolouration as well as numbness and pins and needles.

Only make enough Elixir cream for a few weeks. It's best to keep it fresh.

Elixir spray

You can also use a gem Elixir as a spray using a small plant spray bottle such as you get in the garden centres, or possibly a perfume atomiser.

Fill the bottle with purified or spring water and add a few drops of the elixir to it. Once it's made you should keep in the fridge.

You can use an elixir spray to treat a room, simply spraying the air as you would with an air freshener. You can also use it as a treat for your plants to improve their health.

An elixir spray can be used as an aura spray in a child's room or for a pet. This is a very safe way to introduce crystal healing without the risk of an actual crystal being swallowed.

An obsidian elixir spray can be very helpful to improve blood circulation, especially for anyone who suffers from cold hands or feet.

An elixir spray can also be a very effective way of working with obsidian to protect your personal space. There are times when the negative energy from other people can make your life extremely uncomfortable, whether it is deliberately directed at you or not. For instance, if you are working with somebody who is very negative, their energy will drain your own energy, and the ability of obsidian to create a shield can be extremely helpful in this case. An elixir spray is one of the ways you can introduce this energy into your personal space if you feel unable to work with the actual crystals or if you want to add to the effects.

Unfortunately, there are also times when the negative energy is directly aimed at you. This can be a problem in your work environment, but it can also be a problem in your home, where you are having trouble either from neighbours or from someone within the home. Again, using an elixir spray of obsidian can create an area of protection for you. You could also add a few drops of aromatherapy oil to the elixir and allow people to assume that you are using your own personalised air freshener.

Healing energies of obsidian

Obsidian is a very grounding and protective energy, helping spiritual growth and giving psychic protection. It is also a wonderful energy for helping heal deep mental and spiritual wounds, helping you deal with changes in life and breaking through energy blockages that are holding you back. It can even help you integrate the dark areas of your nature, controlling them and helping you turn them into positive areas and to tap into your unused abilities.

It is a very powerful crystal for helping you deal with mental stress and protecting you from negative energy from other people, helping shield you from the problems and stress that are caused by others and from outside influences.

Obsidian is a very powerful and very protective crystal energy, and it can work very fast, which means that it should be used with care if you are working with it to release long held negative emotions.

It shows no mercy when revealing the truth and can expose weaknesses and personality flaws that you have hidden from yourself. This is a very healing process, very liberating and cathartic, but it can be quite difficult to deal with and a shock to the system.

Spiritual healing

Obsidian is a very powerful root chakra crystal, and so very helpful for grounding you when you are involved in spiritual or healing work. It is considered to be very

21

protective and can help you link with the energy of the Earth, it is a powerful crystal to work with when you require psychic protection.

Because of the nature of obsidian - it often has a very glassy lustre - it has been used to create scrying mirrors in many cultures over the centuries. The Mayan priests of the God Tetzcatlipoca (smoking Mirror) used obsidian mirrors to predict the future. Many people still use a scrying mirror today for divination and when working with the spirit realm and although you can use any mirror for scrying, most people do prefer a black mirror, and a natural polished obsidian is the preferred choice.

Obsidian is also considered to aid spiritual communication, and is often used to help you find your spirit guide or to strengthen meditation. An obsidian mirror or highly polished sphere or piece of obsidian is again a very useful tool for meditation, as you can focus your thoughts into the obsidian allowing your mind to drift free. If you are working with obsidian for meditation is best to complete your session by focusing on some clear quartz.

Obsidian is often used in healing and to help with past life healing, especially when you are carrying negative energies from past lives. When working with obsidian for past life healing effects can be extremely strong and fast, showing no mercy when opening your eyes to your own flaws and weaknesses.

This can be a very uncomfortable and even traumatic process, as it can force you to face some unpleasant truths. But it is also a very healing process, allowing you to see what is holding you back so that you can deal with the problems and move on in your life. Have some rose quartz and clear quartz close to you, so that you can work with these calming loving energies after your session. They can help restore your balance and strengthen your self-confidence after the healing process

Although obsidian is normally associated with the root chakra, it also has a link with the third eye chakra, where it can help with insight, either with resolving past life issues or finding the purpose of your place in this life.

Placing a piece of obsidian on the third eye can help when you need to make decisions concerning career choices finances or major relationships. It can also help when you are trying to make decisions about health issues. Obsidian is an excellent energy when you are at periods of change in your life such as changing career, from education to work, moving to a new home or even a new area, or making other major changes in your life where you need to remain flexible.

The deep spiritual healing that obsidian can bring, although at first uncomfortable, can mean that you then feel that you want to make major changes in your life and working with obsidian on your third eye chakra can help you in this decision-making.

Mental and emotional healing

If you are working with obsidian for deep, mental healing, try working with snowflake, mahogany, lamellen or apache tear obsidians first, they have a gentler energy than pure black obsidian, which can be a bit unforgiving.

It's a good idea to have some clear quartz or rose quartz to place close to you after your healing with obsidian, to calm and restore your balance.

Obsidian is also a wonderful crystal to help you overcome a severe shock or trauma, or a deep seated fear. It helps open up the mind and clear blocks that are holding you back or creating an obsession, even helping you deal with an obsessive nature.

It can help expand your mind, making it a wonderful energy for times of change in life. It helps you open your mind to new ideas, let go of a past that is holding you back, or allowing you to let go of beliefs that are restricting your ability to grow.

This makes it a very good crystal for those times when change is inevitable or desirable.

- Moving on from education to work life.
- Changing career or searching for a new job
- Moving into a new relationship
- Moving on from an old relationship
- Moving home, city or country

Obsidian is also a very protective crystal when you are dealing with negative energy from other people, which can cause great distress, both mentally and emotionally. Everybody comes across people, whose energy is incompatible with your own. Some people, no matter how much you try, you just don't like. That's normal, our energy fields are very sensitive, and we simply may be unable to get along with another person.

But unfortunately there are times in life when the negative energy coming from another person is much more focused, directed straight at you and it can cause you distress, even harm, leading to stress, depression, and if allowed to continue, physical illness.

It can be very difficult to see how you can deal with this kind of attack or affect. The best thing is to be able to remove yourself from it but that can be very difficult when the source of the attack is a co-worker or even a manager, or if the problem is at home, either inside the family itself or with neighbours. Changing career, moving home, or breaking up a family are very drastic actions and are normally a very last resort.

Obsidian can help deflect and protect you from the negative energy that is directed at you. It can create a shield that can defend you from the depressing, counter-productive, unenthusiastic, disapproving or pessimistic energies that are flowing your way.

It won't change the person who is producing the negative energy but it will lessen their ability to have an effect on you, because you will be sheltering behind the shield.

You will have to have the obsidian actually with you at the time to produce this protection. Wearing or carrying a piece is one way, but you can also work with actual pieces - tumbled, natural or carved. Place them to form a shield between you and the source of the negative energy, for instance, on your desk at the border where that person interacts with you.

If you have problems with your neighbours, you can place pieces of obsidian along the adjoining wall, or at the front or back of the house where their energy would enter your home. You can also work with an elixir spray to protect your personal space. Of course, you can combine any of these methods if you feel that you need more protection.

Physical healing

Physically, obsidian can help ease pain, energy blocks or tension. It is considered to help accelerate the healing of wounds and to improve the circulation, making it a very helpful crystal for anyone who suffers from cold hands and feet, and the problems connected with Reynard's disease, where the blood circulation to the fingers and toes can be temporarily blocked causing discolouration discomfort, tingling and pins and needles.

It is even considered to help extreme problems such as hardening of the arteries, for instance the problems caused by smoking.

It can help reduce pain, which makes it a popular crystal for those suffering from arthritis or joint problems.

Obsidian is also considered to help ease the shock caused by injury and help reduce bleeding also accelerating the actual healing of wounds. An elixir or elixir cream can be very helpful when treating wounds.

The ability of obsidian to let you see the unpleasant truths that might be holding you back can also help with physical healing by allowing you to accept a problem and move on with the healing process. The very fact that you are dealing with spiritual or emotional problems can also help relieve physical problems such as problems with the digestion or tension headaches.

Obsidian can also be a very useful crystal when you are living with a chronic illness such as ME/chronic fatigue syndrome or fibromyalgia. One of the most difficult things to deal with in these illnesses is the attitude of other people who simply believe that you should 'pull yourself together' or that your illness is 'all in the mind'.

This kind of attitude from friends, medical practitioners and sometimes family, can make it very difficult to focus on improving your health and learning to live with a chronic illness. The ability of obsidian to give you a shield against the negative energy coming from other people can be very useful in these cases.

Varieties of obsidian

There are a number of varieties of obsidian, and they have slightly different effects. Some are more gentle than others, some better for intuitive work or meditation. The form of obsidian that you choose is entirely down to personal choice. Simply pick a piece that attracts you. You may also choose to work with a variety of different obsidians in different situations. Personally I like to wear snowflake obsidian and lamellan obsidian but I have black and mahogany obsidian around me as I work.

You will come across some blue and green obsidian, and natural obsidians in these shades are very beautiful and very rare. Generally, brightly coloured obsidians are man-made. They are glass, but they are not glass formed in the energy of a volcano.

Black obsidian

This is one of the most powerful obsidians, an excellent crystal for meditation and scrying, especially in the form of a

mirror or a sphere. It can release emotions very fast, not allowing you any place to hide from the truth and the real you, so it can be quite difficult to work with at first unless you are experienced. If you have deep emotional and spiritual healing issues you should work with the guidance of a healer, as this crystal can look deeply into your emotions and old trauma, providing powerful healing.

It is also a very grounding and protective energy, a powerful protector against negative energies or psychic attack and can be worked with keep you safe from curses as well as being able to keep you spiritually grounded.

Snowflake Obsidian

Although obsidian does not form crystals, snowflake obsidian occurs when there are small grey feldspar crystals forming inside the black obsidian.

This lovely form of obsidian is one of the gentler energies in this family. It is very calming and soothing and helps gently release emotional blocks that might be holding you back in life, allowing you to move on from a deep-rooted pattern of behaviour that is making growth difficult.

It is also one of the stronger obsidians if you want to improve the circulation (also mahogany obsidian).

It is a very balancing energy for Mind, Body and Spirit, and is very protective against other people's negative energies. It is the type of obsidian that I tend to reach for when clients are concerned with their career, looking for new employment, dealing with redundancy or starting their career after leaving education

Apache Tear

Legend says that these pebbles of translucent black obsidian are the solidified tears of Apache women mourning the massacre of their warriors, and it is said that anyone who owns an Apache Tear need never cry again. They are often carried as good luck charms and are said to have great powers of protection.

Apache tear is also known as smoky obsidian and is translucent when held up to the light.

Like all obsidian, it is a powerfully protective crystal but it is gentler than black obsidian, and although it will still help you bring up the negative emotions and fears that are holding you back, it will do it more gently and slowly than black obsidian, giving you time to deal with the emotions,

It is a wonderful crystal for protecting the aura.

It is considered to improve the circulation, even in extreme cases and is also used for alleviating pain and healing wounds when placed next to the skin. It is a good crystal for helping you deal with fear or panic or a sudden shock.

Rainbow Obsidian

Rainbow obsidian has beautiful delicate, almost mystical iridescent patterns within it and it is a powerful protector, but is one of the gentler obsidians to work with.

It has a very spiritual energy and can help you let go of old loves, healing the heart chakra and releasing old hurts that people in your life have left you with.

It is said to protect from negative energies, both your own and those of others, and to help you change negatives into positives, making it wonderful for times of change. It helps open you up again if old pain has closed you in on yourself.

Sheen obsidian

Rare Sheen Obsidian can be a gold sheen or a silver sheen. Both colours are very good for scrying and meditation.

Gold sheen obsidian can help you heal from emotional injuries, taking you deep into the root of a problem and showing you what healing is needed, although other crystals will be used for the actual healing. It can help those who suffer from an entrenched pessimism and allow you to dismiss feelings of futility.

Silver sheen obsidian can help you deal with repressed emotions, it can work as a mirror to your inner being. It can help strengthen your patience and give you a better sense of perception, allowing you to deal with problems logically and strengthening your perseverance so that you can deal with problems that have been hidden for a long time.

Sheen Obsidian is a powerful protector against all types of negative energy and is very protective against psychic attack.

It is a very helpful crystal for times when the healing process has reached a block, as it can help move it on again

Lamellen obsidian

Lamellen obsidian is also called midnight lace obsidian and is a relatively new form of obsidian in the marketplace.

It is found mainly in Eastern Europe and is quite limited in availability. The blades of obsidian run through an otherwise transparent gem, forming a pattern of clear and black lines, which has led to the name midnight lace obsidian. It can also create a beautiful translucent brown gemstone.

I find that it is a gentle form of obsidian, but is very good at helping you move forward in dealing with a problem.

Mahogany Obsidian

This is another of the more gentle energies of obsidian.

It is a good crystal to work with when you are dealing with people who undermine you and try to damage your confidence with insults or even false accusations.

It can help strengthen your resolve, revitalizing you and helping give you new drive to move forward with a project, a plan or with life in general. It helps give you strength in difficult times and can be a very stabilizing energy

Chakra healing

Ancient Indian Sanskrit texts teach us of the Chakra system. They tell of centres of energy in the human body, with seven major points arranged along the line of the spine.

During our daily life, they can become unbalanced, which can hinder the flow of energy throughout the body. Over time this can contribute to illness or emotional upset.

We are very complex systems, and many illnesses cannot be treated simply. All parts of our body interact with others and we should treat ourselves as a whole rather than as a collection of parts.

Keeping our energy system in balance is a vital part of maintaining our general well-being.

In Eastern Yogic texts, the chakras are visualised as lotus flowers, with the petals and fine roots of the flower distributing the life force – or Prana – throughout the physical body and converting the energy into chemical, hormonal and cellular changes.

The vibration of crystals can harmonise the Chakras and allow the energy to flow freely again, which is why it can be helpful to use a charka healing layout as well as the more direct use of a crystal or crystals that are specifically linked to the problem or illness that you want to treat.

Different crystals and colour, and the vibrational energy of the colour are linked to each charka, and for this type of healing, the colour is an important part of the choice that you make.

Although obsidian is a powerful root chakra crystal, it is also a very useful crystal for the Third Eye chakra, especially when you're looking for answers to questions.

The Root Chakra (1st)

Maladhara – Mal = root : Adhara = support, vital part

Also known as the earth charka the 'root of our support'

Located at the base of the spine, situated where your body meets the earth when you sit.

This is the chakra that controls our ability to be grounded. It is associated with physical energy and physical health. If this is blocked you can feel anxious, insecure, frustrated. Physically it can cover osteoarthritis, obesity, problems with the feet and legs, haemorrhoids and constipation and chronic long term illnesses.

Colours: Red, black, dark brown

Gland: Testes/Ovaries
Sense: Smell
Colour: Red, dark brown or black
Intake: Protein
Element: Earth
Oils: Patchouli; musk; cedarwood, myrrh
Symbol: 4 crimson petal lotus flower, around a yellow square containing a downward pointing triangle
Masculine – Yang

Areas of effect

This is the chakra that controls our ability to be grounded. In fact, the nerve bundle at this chakra resembles a massive root system, it leaves the spine and runs down both legs as the sciatic nerve to the heels and the tip of your toes.

It is associated with physical energy and physical health, survival, being grounded, health, vitality and fitness. It is the chakra for the spinal column, the feet and legs, large intestine and kidneys and of course, the sciatic nerve.

Balance

When the root chakra is balanced you are grounded. You feel a sense of security and stability, a feeling of 'being at home', both with yourself and your past, it gives you a trust in the natural order of things. You have energy and good general health

It is very important to have this chakra balanced. There is a tendency to concentrate on the higher chakras at the expense of the root, sacral and solar plexus, but it's very important to remember that we are 'whole' beings and therefore need to keep the 'whole' system in balance.

The root charka is directly linked to the crown chakra and is the foundation of your entire energy system. It is the chakra that gives you a solid base in reality and keeps you grounded as well as being vital for physical energy and general good health.

Imbalance

When there is imbalance in this chakra, it can manifest in problems with food – either obesity or underweight, greed in food and in general. You can feel anxious, insecure, frustrated. It can cover osteoarthritis, problems with the feet and legs, haemorrhoids and constipation, problems with the bones and teeth.

It can also cause low energy problems or chronic fatigue or mental lethargy as well as an inability to find inner stillness or peace. Imbalance can also cause excess worry about security or money fears, leading you to crave security and rigid rules and boundaries to an almost addictive degree.

You have to pay special attention to the base chakra in any case of chronic ill-health – for instance M.E. – or in cases of lack of security. It is literally your base and whatever else you want to achieve, you must be strong physically.

The Third Eye Chakra (6th)

Ajna = command

Also known as the brow or intuitive chakra

Located between and just above the eyes.

It is associated with intuition, psychic ability, energies of the spirit and the elimination of selfish attitudes. If it is out of balance you may feel afraid of success, non-assertive or the opposite, egotistical. Physically it can lead to headaches, nightmares, eye problems and poor vision or neurological disturbances.

Gland: pituitary
Sense: light, sixth sense
Intake: air
Element: mind and light
Oils: violet, hyacinth
Symbol: a white circle containing a downward pointing triangle and held by two large lotus petals – one to each side
Feminine - Yin

Areas of effect

The third eye chakra is associated with intuition, psychic ability, wisdom, energies of the spirit and the elimination of selfish attitudes, the eyes, base of the skull, sinus, mental and emotional balance.

Balance

When is it in balance you have imagination, clear vision, you are able to interpret experiences accurately. You are highly intuitive, have a good memory, emotional balance and mental organisation.

Psychic abilities are available when the third eye chakra is properly balanced and it can enable the talents of artists, healers and therapists to blossom.

A balanced third eye chakra gives you the power to override your logical, intellectual responses to a situation and follow your instincts, thereby allowing your 'true self' to shine.

Imbalance

If it is out of balance you may feel afraid of success, non-assertive or the opposite, egotistical. It can manifest in nightmares, hallucinations, inability to concentrate and poor memory or learning difficulties.

You rationalise everything too much, wanting logical reasons and explanations rather than being able to accept the wonder of the world.

Physically it can lead to headaches, eye problems, glaucoma and poor vision or neurological disturbances.

Obsidian jewellery.

There are times when you will want to work with obsidian over long periods of time, for instance, when you are working with the gemstone to help protect you from negative energy or to help you deal with circulation problems or pain.

If you are working with your obsidian for this kind of protection you will need to have it with you during the day, and although you can carry a piece or keep a piece close to you as you work, it is often easier and more convenient to simply wear your obsidian.

Obsidian has been a popular gemstone throughout history for making knives blades or mirrors but has also long been used for jewellery.

A dark coloured or black stone is very unisex, and therefore obsidian is one of the gemstones that have been used for men's jewellery as well as traditional women's jewellery.

In modern jewellery, obsidian is normally found as cabochons set into silver in Artisan jewellery or as bead jewellery, and the most popular forms are black obsidian and snowflake obsidian, valued in the jewellery trade for its unusual beauty - and of course, it is fashionably monochrome!

If you want to work with other forms of obsidian, you should look for pieces created for their healing energies rather and metaphysical outlets than just as pieces of fashion jewellery.

Although you will find pieces of obsidian set as quite ornate jewellery, you can also find it in simple settings, or even on cords as unisex pendants. It can also be set into tie clips or cufflinks, Signet rings or simple bracelets.

You'll also find obsidian arrowheads fashioned into 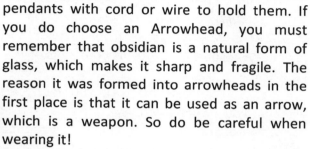 pendants with cord or wire to hold them. If you do choose an Arrowhead, you must remember that obsidian is a natural form of glass, which makes it sharp and fragile. The reason it was formed into arrowheads in the first place is that it can be used as an arrow, which is a weapon. So do be careful when wearing it!

It is perfectly safe to wear obsidian over long periods of time, and it is a lovely energy to work close to the body. So it is a perfect crystal to choose as your signature piece of jewellery to wear regularly, or even daily.

Personal healing patterns

As with any healing crystal, the obsidian crystal must be inside your own energy field (about arms length) in order to be able to work on balancing you.

That is why it is easy to wear your obsidian set into jewellery, to carry a piece in your pocket or keep it under your pillow.

But you can also place the obsidian either on you or around you when you want to spend time actually concentrating on healing and balancing your energy.

A healing pattern of natural Clear Quartz points surrounding the body, with a obsidian polished stone placed at the root chakra can be an extremely powerful healing pattern for grounding and for dealing with problems with the feet and legs or pelvis.

You can also place an obsidian polished stone, especially a sheen obsidian, on the third eye, surrounded by this clear quartz pattern to improve psychic ability, or to help with decision-making.

This general Natural Clear Quartz point healing pattern can be used with many different crystals actually placed on the body – either a single crystal for a very specific healing energy or a range of crystals creating a healing recipe.

The general healing pattern of quartz points works because of the ability of natural quartz points to direct energy, either negative energy out of your energy field or positive energy into your energy field. The energy flows in the direction of the natural point.

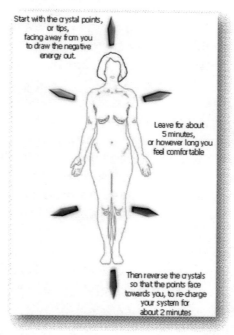

Start with the crystal points, or tips, facing away from you to draw the negative energy out.

Leave for about 5 minutes, or however long you feel comfortable

Then reverse the crystals so that the points face towards you, to re-charge your system for about 2 minutes

Find a time and place where you can relax and will be undisturbed, ideally for about 20 minutes.

Make sure that the energy you will be directing into your energy field is fresh and pure, don't set up next to the TV, computer or close to electricity pylons. Wear comfortable clothing - you don't want to be distracted by an irritatingly tight waistband!

You might want to light some aromatherapy candles or play some gentle music to help create a bubble of relaxations and peace,

Place the points facing away from the body to draw negative energy away – leave for about 5 minutes.

Then reverse the points to face in towards the body for about 2 minutes, to draw fresh positive energy into the energy field.

Remove the crystals and relax, allowing your energy field to absorb the fresh healing energy.

Obsidian can also be laid on the body for healing, placing it either directly on, or in the general area of the part of the body that requires healing. For chakra healing, this would be on the root chakra or the third eye chakra

A healing pattern with obsidian can be very helpful when you want to ease general physical pain, improve blood circulation or ease tension, especially the kind of tension caused by the negative energy from other people. This can make it a very helpful healing pattern when you've had a stressful day at work.

Forming a healing circle of obsidian gems is also a very calming healing pattern and works well with meditation. Simply select your crystals and place them in a circle surrounding you.

Healing your environment

Crystals can be used to 'heal' your environment as well as your health and emotions. Not only do they create a beautiful decorative focus for a room, they can actively help to reduce the effects of emotional stress.

In general, it is better to use pieces of rough, unpolished crystals rather than tumbled crystals for environmental use as they will spread their effect further - throughout the room rather than just within your own personal aura. In this case, larger pieces will have a 'larger' effect, as their radius of influence will be wider. Although a bowl of small tumbled obsidian can help create sense of safety and security in a room

When you want to cleanse the energy in a larger area, you have to work with larger crystals that can spread their energies further.

Obsidian is considered to be a very protective energy, and pieces of obsidian placed around the entrance to your home can help create a stable, balanced energy, drawing in positive energy and good luck into your life.

All obsidians can be very helpful when you need protection from the negative energy from other people, whether this is a deliberate attack or is just an accidental affect of their own negativity.

Obsidian will literally create a shield for you, so that the energy cannot get through to you and cause problem in your own energy field.

You can either wear a piece of obsidian as jewellery to create your own personal shield, or place some pieces of obsidian as an energy wall between you and the problem.

So if the problem is with a co-worker, put some obsidian tumbled stones or natural pieces on the area where that person's energy field intersects your own – along your desk, at the wall between two offices, at the doorway where they enter your space.

If you have a problem with neighbours, you can again place a line of obsidian between you and them along the joining wall of your houses, at the front or back of the house if they live opposite.

Carvings or jewellery work just as well as natural or polished pieces, and they will attract less attention from a sceptic, you don't want to give them any extra ammunition against you, especially as you now have your own stock of missiles!

An elixir spray of obsidian can be a very useful way of protecting your personal area, as again it can be unobtrusive with can be important when you want to try and deal with the problem quietly rather than bringing it out into the open.

Add some aromatherapy oil to your elixir spray to create your own personal air freshener or perfume.

Juniper berry, pine, cypress, frankincense and myrrh are essential oils that are traditionally considered to help cleanse negative energy, although you can add any scent that you would prefer to surround yourself with.

Cleansing crystals

A new crystal should always be cleansed before you use it for healing. This is not actually to clean dirt from it, but the unwanted energy it will have gathered from other people.

You should also cleanse your crystals between specific healing sessions to avoid transferring negative energies and you should cleanse them as a general habit when you feel that they are less affective or on a regular basis. Learn to trust your instincts, you will learn to feel when they need cleansing and recharging.

There are many ways suggested for cleansing but care should be taken before you decide on which method to use. Some crystals would be destroyed by water, while others would fade in sunlight - amethyst, rose quartz and aventurine can all be badly affected by too much sunlight.

Personally I prefer to avoid some of the other methods that are sometimes recommended.

Placing a crystal in salt water or sitting it directly in salt can be very damaging for some crystals. A salt solution, can penetrate some crystal structures, making the stone cloudy or discolouring it. Sitting some crystals in salt would destroy them altogether. For instance, placing an Opal on a bed of salt would draw the water from it, changing it from an Opal gemstone into a much less valuable piece of chalcedony.

I also prefer to avoid burying a crystal. Apart from the obvious danger of not being able to find it again, there is the risk that the soil conditions will damage the crystal. For instance, your soil may be too acid for some gemstones.

In crystal healing, we are working with the energies of crystals and we should respect them and take care of the crystals we have chosen so that they will continue to work with us for many years.

An Amethyst bed or druze is a very useful crystal for helping to cleanse other crystals. Simply place your other crystals gently onto the surface of the natural points and allow the Amethyst to focus the negative energy away from them. Leave them for approximately 3 to 4 hours. This method is gentle enough for any of your crystals, even those set into jewellery, although you do need to take care that soft gems will not be scratched by the amethyst, which is a hard crystal (7 on the MOHs scale). Obsidian is approximately 5 – 5.5 on the MOHs scale

Do not leave the crystals on the amethyst too long, as amethyst is very energising and other crystals can begin to take on the energy of the amethyst. If you do leave them too long, set your crystals aside to allow them to recover their own energy.

You can also use sea salt to cleanse the negative energy from your obsidian. You can find sea salt at most supermarkets.

Place the dry sea salt into a clear glass bowl. It is important to use clear glass as you do not want to introduce colour energy into the cleansing.

Sit a smaller clear glass bowl in the sea salt so that it is surrounded by the salt.

Place your obsidian (or other crystals) into the second bowl so that it is surrounded by but not touching the salt. Leave it for three to four hours.

You can reuse the salt for many months for cleansing, just cover it so that it doesn't get too dusty but never use it for cooking once you have been cleansing crystals, you don't want to ingest the negative energy.

If you're comfortable with dowsing with a pendulum you can cleanse your crystals in this way as well. Just ask your pendulum to remove the negative energy from your crystals and then hold it over the crystals and let it move as it wants until it comes naturally to a halt. This will make  sense if you are an experienced dowser - if you've never worked with a pendulum - it'll make no sense at all!

You should cleanse your crystals when you 'feel' that they need it, there are no timetables for this. A crystal that absorbs negative energy - for instance snowflake obsidian or quartz crystal kept beside a TV - will require quite frequent cleansing, at least once a month, but weekly would be better. So will a crystal that you are using to absorb pain, such as malachite, which for severe pain should be cleansed daily. But you may feel that other crystals only need cleansing after a number of months, in fact, a citrine pendant worn every day, may only need cleansing every six months.

Use your intuition - you can tell when your crystal is no longer as effective as it was. Until you get the 'feel' for them, a good guideline is about once a month.

Moon Magic

Obsidian loves the energy of the moon and leaving it in the moonlight can be a very powerful cleanser. It can also be a powerful way of charging your crystal for a specific healing task.

The different phases of the moon have different spiritual energies.

The new moon is for new beginnings, starting new ventures. It's also the time that is recommended for jobhunting and obsidian is perfect for those times in your life, as it helps keep you positive and encourages you to be flexible at times of change.

The waxing moon between the new and full moon is considered to be the energy of getting things done, such as dealing with matters of courage and luck, wealth or success.

The full moon is very cleansing and energising, perfect for clearing your crystals of unwanted energy once you have finished a healing task.

The waning moon between the full and new moon is a very good time to cleanse crystals if you have been working with them in dealing with a lot of negative energies such as serious illness, addictions or negative emotions, as it is a very good energy for banishing that negativity. So this phase of the moon is good if you are working with your obsidian to protect you from negativity.

The dark of the moon, the three days before the new moon, is traditionally a time for recuperation, rest and meditation.

When you want to work with your crystals for a specific task, you can choose the right phase of the moon to suit the energy you require and charge your obsidian with that energy before you start your healing work.

About the Author

From a long line of healers on the West Coast of Ireland, Brenda has worked with healing crystals and a dowsing pendulum for almost 20 years and is a member of the British Society of Dowsers.

She regularly gives talks and classes on dowsing, vibrational therapies, crystal healing and colour healing as well as writing books, articles and well known series of Core Information charts on a number of alternative therapies.

you can contact her at: brenda@healing-earth.co.uk
website: www.healing earth.co.uk

If you have enjoyed this book, please could you leave feedback at Amazon

Whilst reasonable care is taken to ensure the accuracy of the information in this publication, no responsibility can be accepted for the consequences of any actions based on any opinions, information or advice found in the publication.

Healing information contained in this publication should not be taken as a substitute for professional medical advice. You should always consult your doctor on serious matters.

44804578R10030

Made in the USA
Lexington, KY
10 September 2015